Sorting and using materials

Peter Riley and Dr Brian Knapp

Curriculum Visions

Science@School

Teacher's Guide
There is a Teacher's Guide available
to accompany this book.

Dedicated Web Site
There is a wealth of supporting
material including videos and activities
available at the Professional Zone,
part of our dedicated web site:

www.CurriculumVisions.com

The Professional Zone
is a subscription zone.

A CVP Book.
First published in 2008

Copyright © 2008 Earthscape

*The rights of Peter Riley and Brian Knapp to be
identified as the authors of this work have been
asserted by them in accordance with the Copyright,
Designs and Patents Act 1988.*

*All rights reserved. No part of this publication may be
reproduced, stored in a retrieval system, or transmitted
in any form or by any means, electronic, mechanical,
photocopying, recording or otherwise, without prior
permission of the publisher and the copyright holder.*

Authors
*Peter Riley, BSc, C Biol, MI Biol, PGCE,
and Brian Knapp, BSc, PhD*

Senior Designer
Adele Humphries, BA, PGCE

Educational Consultant
*Jan Smith (former Deputy Head of Wellfield School,
Burnley, Lancashire)*

Editor
Gillian Gatehouse

Designed and produced by
EARTHSCAPE

Printed in China by
WKT Co., Ltd

**Curriculum Visions Science@School
Volume 1C Sorting and using materials**
*A CIP record for this book is available
from the British Library.*
ISBN: 978 1 86214 255 8

Picture credits
All pictures are from the Earthscape and
ShutterStock collections.

*This product is manufactured from sustainable
managed forests. For every tree cut down at least one
more is planted.*

Cotton comes from a cotton plant.
Cotton is used to make clothes.

 # Contents

Weblink: www.curriculumvisions.com

Things around us

There are lots of things around us.

Here are some things you may have at school.

pencil

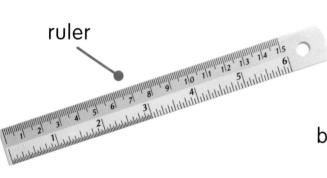

ruler

pen

book

What other things have you got at school?

Weblink: www.curriculumvisions.com

Here are some things
you may have at home.

comb

mug

spoon

fork

knife

plate

What other things have you got at home?

Weblink: www.curriculumvisions.com

Materials

We use materials to make things.

Everything is made from something.
We say it is made from a material.

There are lots of materials
to make things with.

We can use wood.

We can use leather.

We can use wool.

We can use plastic.

We can use glass.

These mugs are
made from plastic.

These pencils are made from wood.

Weblink: www.curriculumvisions.com

These old boots are made from leather.

The shirt is made from cotton. The spoon is made from metal. The tumbler is made from glass.

spoon

shirt

tumbler

Can you think of more materials?

Weblink: www.curriculumvisions.com

Properties

Every material is different.

If every material was the same, we would not be able to make many different things.

Here are some of the differences.

Some plastic things are soft and shiny.

soft plastic toy

mobile phone

Some plastic things are smooth and hard.

Metal things are hard and shiny.

metal spoon

metal fork

metal knife

dough

Dough is dull and soft.

Weblink: www.curriculumvisions.com

Shampoo is runny and foamy.

Sandpaper is bendy and rough.

teapot

wooden bowl

Wood is dull and hard.

Pottery is hard and waterproof.

Is the teapot shiny or dull? Is it hard or soft?

Sorting

You can sort materials in lots of ways.

shell

Many things feel the same. They may be soft. They may be smooth. They may be shiny.

Here we have grouped some things by how they feel – hard, soft, smooth and rough.

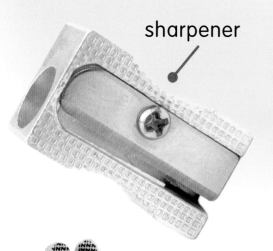

sharpener

These materials are hard.

paperclip

These materials are soft.

bread

gloves

Weblink: www.curriculumvisions.com

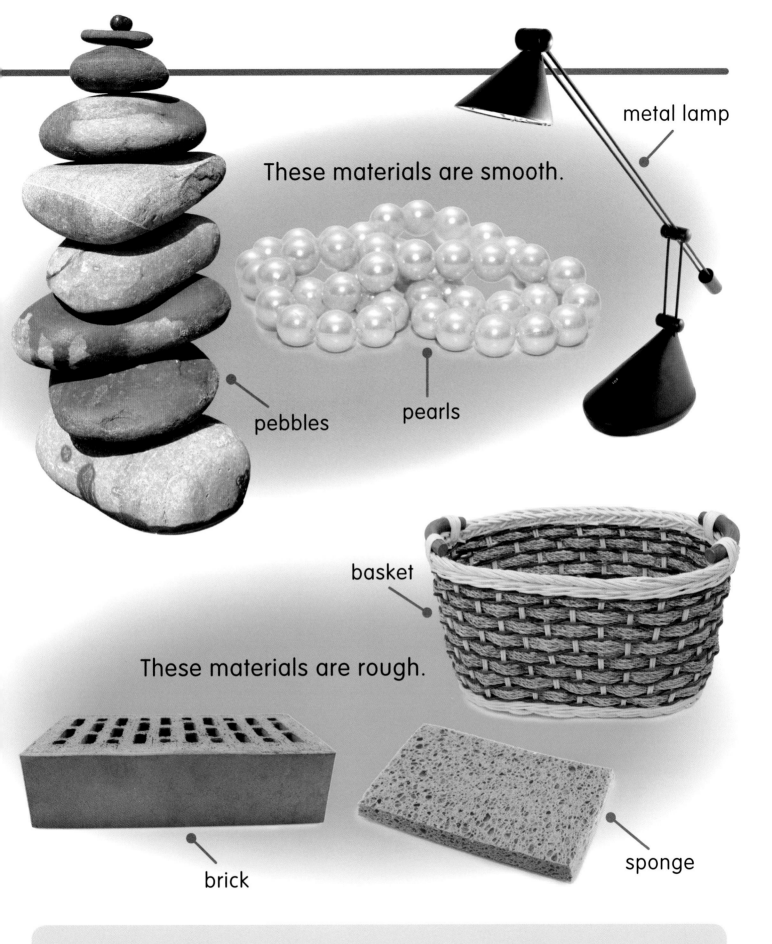

These materials are smooth.

metal lamp

pebbles

pearls

basket

These materials are rough.

brick

sponge

Can you sort these materials into some different groups?

Waterproof

Waterproof materials keep water out.

Waterproof materials do not let water go through them.

You can stay dry under waterproof materials when it rains.

Some materials let water pass through them. You can get wet underneath them when it rains.

Most clothes are not waterproof.
We clean them by getting them wet.

Hair is not waterproof, but skin is waterproof.

Water stays on the skin of this apple.
The apple skin is waterproof.

Weblink: www.curriculumvisions.com

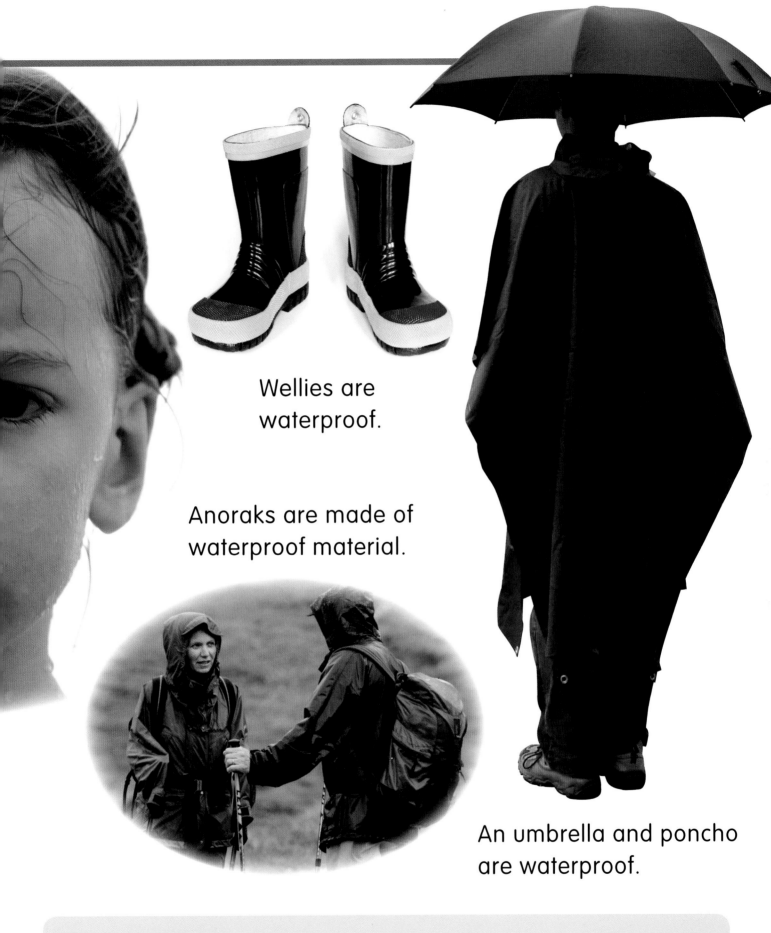

Wellies are waterproof.

Anoraks are made of waterproof material.

An umbrella and poncho are waterproof.

How could you test a material to see if it is waterproof?

Weblink: www.curriculumvisions.com

Stretchy and springy

Some materials will get bigger when you pull them.

Stretchy materials get bigger when you pull them, and stay that way.

Many materials get bigger when we pull them, but then go back into shape when we let them go.

These are springy materials.

Bubble gum is stretchy but not springy.

trampoline

Trampolines are springy.

These are springy bands. They are made of rubber.

This safety pin is made of a springy metal.

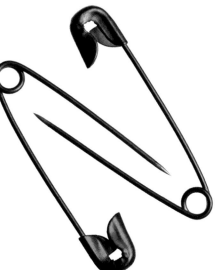

These coils of steel are called springs.

A luggage holder is made of springy rubber.

Can you name some things that are stretchy?

Bendy and brittle

Not all materials will bend.

Many materials will bend. Some will bend a lot.

A few materials will not bend at all. They will break.

These are called brittle materials.

This toy car was made by bending wire.

Car cleaning materials are bendy.

bendy sponge

bendy bucket

bendy hose

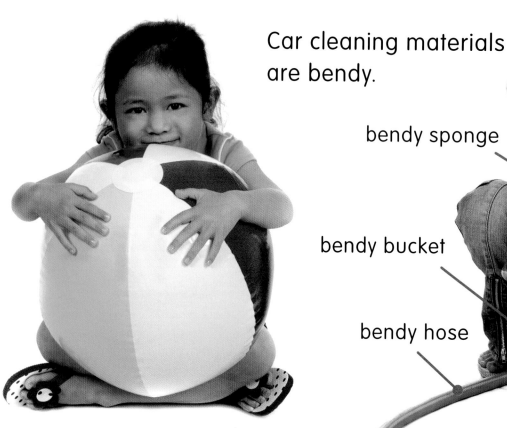

A plastic ball is bendy.

A sheet of glass will not bend.
It breaks when a stone hits it.

A plastic bag
is bendy.

chocolate Easter egg

Chocolate will not bend.
It is brittle.

bar of chocolate

What other bendy and brittle materials can you think of?

Weblink: www.curriculumvisions.com

Magnetic and transparent

Some materials, like magnets and glass, are special.

A magnet is a material that is pulled towards iron and steel. A magnet does not pull other materials, such as wood or stone.

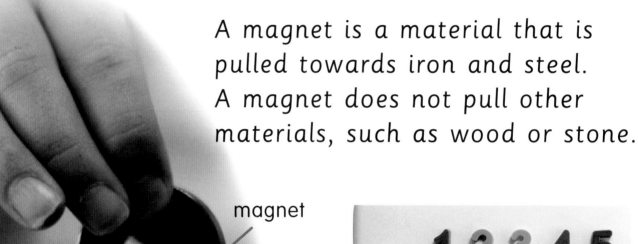

magnet

steel

This magnet is picking up pieces of steel.

Magnetic letters hold on to a steel fridge door.

How could you test paper to see if it was a magnetic material?

Weblink: www.curriculumvisions.com

You can see through glass.

Glass is called a transparent material.

You can see through the glass in a window.

A magnifying glass is a special shape of glass that lets you see things bigger.

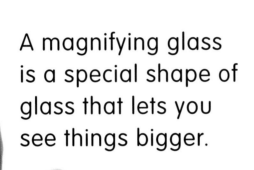

You can see the milk in this glass.

**Look through this book.
Do most materials let light through them?**

Weblink: www.curriculumvisions.com

Using materials

If we know what materials do, we know where to use them.

Look around you.

There are many materials.

This is because people have chosen the best materials for the job.

Cane is bendy and is used to make baskets.

Brick is strong and is used to make walls.

brick wall

Weblink: www.curriculumvisions.com

Wood is hard and smooth and used to make tables, boxes and beds.

Steel is a strong material and is used for making cars.

Is glass useful for making trousers?

Words to learn

Cotton

A material made from hairs on cotton seeds.

Dough

A mixture of flour and water that is used to make bread.

Foamy

Lots of tiny bubbles joined together.

Iron

A hard metal used for making things that are strong, like garden gates.

Leather

A material made from the tough skin of a cow. It is used for things like shoes and footballs.

Pebble

A small, smooth, round stone.

Plastic

A material made from oil.

Pottery

A material made from baked clay. It is waterproof.

Steel

A tough, hard, shiny metal that is used to make things such as cars and bicycles.

Weblink: www.curriculumvisions.com

Index

Weblink: www.curriculumvisions.com